what if you met a Knight

jan adkins
scribe and illuminator

Roaring Brook Press
New Milford, Connecticut

You know all about knights, right? You've seen plenty of them in movies and books.

Best of all, you know about King Arthur and the Round Table at Camelot, with seats for the best knights in the world: Sir Lancelot, Sir Gawain, Sir Tristan, Sir Bors, and a lot of other handsome guys with long, curly hair wearing polished armor. They were loyal, brave, trustworthy, kind, fair, pure of heart, and cram-full of chivalry, the code of knightly conduct. Very nice fellas. Their business was adventure.

There was plenty of adventure to go around. The knights carried swords as big as parking meters and toured the countryside on truck-sized horses. They rescued fair maidens, found Holy Grails, put down evil giants, and did some pest control—slaying troublesome dragons.

Often they would meet an evil false knight and challenge the cad to a joust. The jousters would ride to opposite sides of a meadow, then wheel and charge at each other with lances like flagpoles. *Whammo!* The less virtuous knight went down like a sack of potatoes!

Naturally, those boys had fair ladies of their own—sweet and delicate women in long gowns, veils, and high pointy hats. Normally valiant knights got cow-eyed around ladies—writing poetry, singing under their castle windows, and dedicating spectacular victories to their ladies' virtue.

It was generally a good life of outdoor fun and high deeds for dedicated heroes.

Sure, you know all about knights.

you know all about knights

For a plain round table, it was more complicated than you might think. There are wild tales about each knight.

Gareth: Gawain's youngest brother, devoted to Lancelot—who later killed him while rescuing Guinevere from burning at the stake.

Bors de Ganis: Arthur's cousin, big and brawny but gentle.

Gaheris: Another Orkney, Gawain's middle brother, once his squire.

Galahad: Perfect in all the sweeter knightly virtues. Lancelot's son, though Lance never married his mum.

Percival: A mama's boy, raised at home with no talk of swords and fighting; an innocent, simple-minded young fellow.

Lancelot: The best of all knights (overlooking that unfortunate business with Queen Guinevere).

Arthur: King and general, but also a knight. Married to Guinevere, whose father sent the round table as a wedding gift. He didn't say where he got it.

Bedivere: One of Arthur's first knights, stayed with him to the messy end.

Tristan: An older knight, good harp player, but famous for running away with his uncle's fiancée, Isolde.

Geraint: Prince of a neighboring kingdom, not very interesting.

Kay: Arthur was once a squire to this older foster brother.

Gawain: Oldest of the Orkney boys (a warrior clan), nephew of Arthur, tough but tempery.

Lamorak: Killed Gawain's father and moved in with his mother, so naturally Gawain killed him later.

What If You Met a Knight?   3

meet the real deal

I apologize if Sir Guy of Wareham doesn't appear especially noble or adventurous. He looks upset and irritable. That's because he has a lot on his mind. Being a knight could be a dismal job. A real knight (the word comes from Old English *cniht,* meaning servant) had real work to do and a lot of mouths to feed—and trouble could ride over the hill at any moment.

Forget jousts and quests and dragons. Sir Guy was caught in the middle between warlords and peasants. When he was made a knight, his warlord assigned a big piece of land to him. As rent, the lord requires that Sir Guy supply a quantity of armed men, gold, work on the lord's projects, and food every year.

Guy has hundreds of peasant families living on his land. He keeps them safe from bandits and raiders, and he manages the land (really a vast farm). In turn, the peasants give Guy part of their crop, a number of days of work, and—when the warlords act up—they become soldiers for a certain number of days.

This arrangement is part of feudalism. Complicated? It was Guy's headache, season by season, to figure out how to supervise his peasants, how to satisfy his warlord, what crops to plant, when to harvest, how much to train his soldier-farmers, and how to bring in enough food and firewood to last through the winter. But Sir Guy was worried about more than that.

Force majeure—"greater force"—is the only law. If other lords or knights want Sir Guy's land or castle, their raiders could strike without warning.

Sickness has been reported in one of Sir Guy's villages. No one knows how illness spreads or what to do about it. "Doctors" are useless; they have no medicine that prevents or cures disease. Often, they make it worse. The sickness in the village could be a mild fever. Or it could be the dreaded Black Plague. Sir Guy knows that just one of Europe's many plagues killed hundreds of thousands, maybe millions. He's worried.

Sir Guy doesn't have long, **curly hair** because he has fleas, just like everyone else.

Late in the day, he may be a little muddled. This is because he drinks gallons of ale and wine. Most of the water supply is infected by human and animal poop. People who drink plain water die. Tea and coffee from boiled water (a little safer) won't be popular for centuries.

His teeth hurt. He will lose most of them in time. There are no dentists. The only way to fix a toothache is to pull the tooth.

Stand upwind of Sir Guy. He smells. Everyone knows that baths are unhealthy. His woolen outer clothes are never washed, and he sleeps in his linen underwear for a week at a time.

Sir Guy **owes money.** His suit of armor and his weapons cost more than one of his peasants could make in years. He is also bound to provide his farmer-soldiers with helmets, shields, and weapons. He needs horses and wagons to move his men and their supplies. He's had to borrow money to outfit his little army.

Tithing means giving the Church a tenth of all his earnings. This is what a good Christian knight must do. On top of that, the priests are thinking of enlarging the local church. They expect him to pay for it.

Writing it all down might have helped, but Sir Guy probably couldn't read; most knights were illiterate. Their records were kept by scribes or priests.

The Christian Church insists that **lending money,** like a bank does today, is immoral. Jews could lend money, and they charged interest: To borrow 100 gold coins, Sir Guy paid back 110 gold coins. Sir Guy owes Jewish lenders a fortune. He hates them for not being Christian. They hate him for hating Jews. It's a bad situation.

Sir Guy's warlord or even (oh, no!) his king might visit his castle. Dozens of officials, priests, wives, children, servants, and courtiers (people who loaf around "noble" courts) would arrive with him. Sir Guy would be expected to provide food, wine and ale, rooms, beds, and entertainment for all of these **houseguests.** They could stay for weeks. The visit could ruin Sir Guy.

Edith is pregnant. Sir Guy married Edith for her dowry (a wedding gift from her family)—land that bordered his lands. His warlord and the peasants are pleased: They want him to have a son to take over the family lands. But he's learned to like Edith. So many mothers die at childbirth or shortly after. Half of all children die before the age of five. Guy is worried for his wife and his baby.

Sir Guy's warlord is bored and has started thinking about holding **games** for Midsummer's Eve. This would require new clothes and traveling to the warlord's castle with pregnant Edith. Sir Guy will be expected to bring servants, scribes, priests, and some of his farmer-soldiers (who should have been tending the crops). Sir Guy will be obliged to fight in mock battles. Sometimes the mock battles aren't so mock. He will certainly be bruised, perhaps injured, even killed. He hopes the warlord will put it off.

Horses are ridiculously expensive. They're great for plowing fields, but they're delicate and require daily attention. They need specially fitted shoes made by a blacksmith several times a year. As a knight, Sir Guy needs a stable full of horses for war and travel. And stable boys and blacksmiths. He is learning to hate horses.

so what about king arthur?

As pretty as Camelot might have been, there isn't a shred of evidence for Arthur and his Round Table. So where did all those tales come from? The south of France.

It had a mild climate, rich fields, and plenty of wine. It also had plenty of wealthy, bored noblemen and gentlewomen drinking the wine. In the fourteenth century (when the importance of knighthood was already fading), they welcomed singing poets called troubadours or minstrels to entertain them with stories that flattered their rich hosts and their romantic fantasies.

The troubadours invented King Arthur and other airy stories. They wove fantastic adventures around folktale characters, magic castles, dragons, and wizards. They might not have known one end of a sword from the other, but they knew how to wow an audience.

They sang about a way knights *should* act, creating a Code of Chivalry. This was the way the lords and ladies saw themselves—virtuous, pious, loyal, helpful, elegant. But it wasn't the way knights *did* act—the Middle Ages were full of betrayal, plots, assassinations, rebellions, and almost constant war. Real knights were more often tough, scheming brutes. At best they were professional warriors eager to fight battles and win glory.

The Code of Chivalry was very sweet, but an ambitious knight went about whacking off arms and heads as often as possible.

 6

Troubadours sang about "courtly love" that placed women on an unreachable pedestal. A good knight dedicated his life to an ideal lady love. According to the troubadours, she should actually be married to someone else, and the knight should never expect more than a smile for his adoration. This kind of love was bittersweet, theoretical, pure. Pure soap opera. Knights thought it was cool. Noble ladies swooned over this foolishness and paid the singers well. Then they went on about their less-than-pure lives of court scandals.

middle ages? in the middle of what?

The Middle Ages were in the middle—between the end of the Roman Empire and the Renaissance, or "rebirth," of the fifteenth century. Knighthood—the need for local warlords to protect local territories—was a natural result of the dark Middle Ages. (They were also called medieval times.)

Rome didn't fall; it moved. In the fourth century, the Christian emperor Constantine shifted the capital of the Roman Empire and most of its forces to the narrow Straits of Bosporus between Europe and Asia. He modestly called the new city Constantinople. It became the center of power for a new "Rome" that was more concerned with Asia than with Europe.

After the capital moved, the provinces of Europe were no longer protected by powerful Roman armies. The vast network of all-weather Roman roads and bridges fell into disrepair. Europe dissolved into a hodgepodge of desperate little kingdoms struggling for survival against Viking raids, local wars, and bandits. It was an age of famines, plagues, dim hopes. We have good reasons to call the Middle Ages the Dark Ages.

The skeleton left from the old Roman Empire was the Rome-based Roman Catholic Church. (The Church in Constantinople became the Eastern Orthodox Church.) Politically, the Roman Catholic Church was weak, but it offered the only thread of communication and unity for hundreds of little European territories.

Chivalry meant more than a code of conduct. It also meant the knightly class, from chevalier (horseman). A warlord's chivalry was the group of knights under him. Chivalry could also mean the agreement giving a knight his land in return for service to his warlord.

not even a little bitty king arthur?

Maybe. A native Briton leader fighting the invading Saxons (from northern Europe) in the fourth or fifth century may have been the model for the tales. This Arthur wouldn't have been a king, but a local warlord, perhaps a leader of cavalry trained by the departed Romans.

Arthur and his warriors (probably tribal chieftains) certainly didn't wear shining armor. They probably had metal helmets and mail shirts with heavy leather collars and armpieces. Each carried a sword, a shield, and a lance about eight feet long. They rode from one place to another on small but sturdy horses without stirrups, but they fought on foot in a group. Afoot, they could defend one another and do more damage to undisciplined individual attackers. A mounted charge wasn't practical unless Arthur's enemy was running away.

Did Arthur become King of England by drawing the magical sword Excalibur from a stone? Puh-*lease*. No one thought of "England" then, or of any nation. Just local territory held by force. The real stories about the real Arthur would surely have been grittier, less polite, bloodier, and more heroic than minstrel's tales.

Camelot would not have been a grand stone palace with lofty towers. It would have been a motte-and-bailey hill fort made of earth and wood. It had a dry ditch (the motte, or moat) around an earthen wall topped by palisades—wooden tree trunks lashed together. The court inside the walls was the bailey. The fort-within-a-fort was the keep, or donjon (using the dungeon for a jail came much later).

In the "great hall" of the keep was an open fireplace on a stone hearth. Chimneys wouldn't be invented for hundreds of years, so smoke would have found its way out through windows and holes in the walls. Everyone ate and lived in this common room. Arthur's warriors would have slept there with the servants and dogs near the fire. No privacy. Arthur may have had his own room at the top of the keep.

DRAWBRIDGE, to make entrance slow and difficult for invaders

The real model for the myth of Arthur was probably a tough, successful warlord of mounted infantry in the western hills of England sometime after the fifth century. His "shining armor" may have been bronze or boiled leather. To inspire such a myth, he must have been an extraordinary leader.

What about Merlin? People believed in magic, then. Our Arthur may have trusted an old man to tell the future or at least give him good advice. The stories of Merlin are from old Irish and Scottish tales of wild forest men with magical powers.

DONJON (later written as dungeon), or keep, the fortress within a fortress, where the warlord, his family, and his soldiers lived

BAILEY, the fortress

PALISADE, a wall of tree trunks surrounding the bailey

MOTTE, or moat, with or without water

What If You Met a Knight?

9

what was feudalism?

Sir Guy always had the uncomfortable feeling that trouble was on the way: Vikings from the north, Muslims from the south, mounted invaders from the east. He lived in a dangerous time. The only way he could defend his land was to join other warriors. Feudalism was a primitive form of government that connected bands of warriors to hold off trouble.

It was a **top-to-bottom** system based on trust. Fealty was the trust and obedience a warlord owed his king. A knight owed the same fealty to his warlord, and peasants owed fealty to their knight. This feudal ladder was wide at the base (peasants—there were a lot of them) and narrow at the pointy top (the king—just one). The person above you was your lord. People below you were your vassals.

Fealty worked both ways. A peasant (sometimes called a serf) owed his lord service as a soldier. And rent, and taxes. In return, the peasant was given a fief, a piece of land or a yearly sum of money. The knight also owed his peasants protection and support. If a peasant lost everything in a fire, his lord was obligated to help him, just as the peasant owed service to his lord if the castle burned.

The feudal ladder could have complicated rungs. A lesser king might owe fealty to a king with more land. A knight could owe fealty to more than one lord. It was a tangled web of obligations, loyalties, traditions, and practical necessities.

KING

EARL

BARON

MARQUIS

PEASANT, or serf

KNIGHT

Scutage, or "shield tax," was a way peasants could buy their way out of army service. The tax paid for a professional soldier. Knights preferred this because peasant soldiers were poorly trained and seldom reliable. If they saw armored knights riding down on them with big swords, they ran. They were peasants, but they weren't stupid.

high-born

low-born

Noble families in the Middle Ages put their faith in breeding. Some dogs were bred for herding sheep and other dogs for hunting. A colt from a strong mare and a fast stallion should be strong and fast. Shouldn't a child from a "noble" family be superior? Nobles were sure kids from a "low" family couldn't be smart or virtuous. They built a high barrier between the high-born and the low-born. Today we try to judge each person by what he or she can accomplish, but in the Middle Ages climbing the ladder was nearly impossible.

POPE

NUN

PRIEST

MONK

another ladder

The Church had its own rungs, starting with monks and priests at the lowest level and rising through bishops and cardinals up to the big holy cheese in Rome, the pope.

Many men and women took holy orders: They became monks and nuns, living lives of prayer and service to others in monasteries or nunneries. Some orders cared for the sick, some for travelers. It was a life of obedience with strict rules, but it was often better than the uncertain life of peasants.

The Church was less interested in breeding than in ability. True, there were few cardinals and virtually no popes who weren't rich, politically influential men. But it was possible for a bright young man or woman of a humble family and no wealth to rise through the ranks of the church to an important position.

what did knights do all day?

Most of the time Sir Guy was a **farmer** worrying about his crops. He decided what, when, and where everyone would plow, plant, and harvest. He needed dozens of crops: wheat for bread, grapes for wine, barley and millet and oats for porridge, hops for beer, vegetables for the table, flax to make linen cloth, apples and pears and cherries for eating fresh and for preserving, berries and nuts and herbs for cooking. The knight was responsible for feeding everyone on his land and everyone who visited.

Sir Guy had very little time for questing and adventure. Life in the Middle Ages was hopping.

Sir Guy was a **rancher** with cows, sheep, goats, pigs, chickens, rabbits, and even pigeons. Rails had to be split from forest wood and post-holes dug and fences constructed to keep the animals from trampling the fields. Herders had to move the animals from one pasture to another. Milkmaids brought in milk from cows, sheep, and goats. Milk went sour in a few days, so Guy needed cheese- and butter-makers to preserve it.

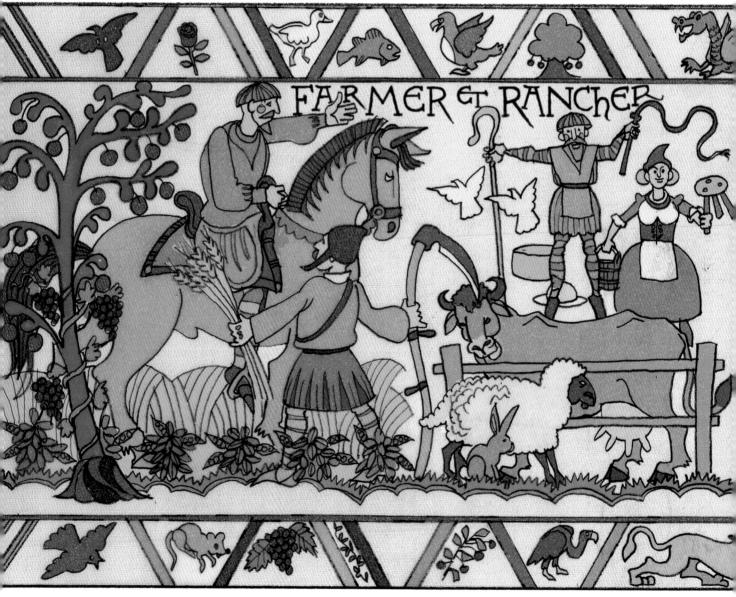

FARMER ET RANCHER

Sir Guy was a **business manager** of cottage industry. In the spring he directed sheep shearing, so the spinners could get busy making wool thread and weavers and dyers could then make cloth. He had tanneries and leather shops for saddles, hinges, reins, boots, hats, buckets, and even armor. He owned the mill that ground the grain for flour. He owned felling axes to cut down trees and big saws to cut them up for lumber. He was a winemaker and a beer brewer. He had beekeepers to keep the bees that pollinated the crops and made honey and wax. He processed animal fat to make tallow candles. He sent village boys to apprentice with blacksmiths, carpenters, weavers, tanners, and other tradesmen in distant provinces to bring back skills to his villages.

He was a **merchant.** Everyone attended Guy's weekly market day. They had to; it was the place where leather workers could trade belts for eggs and beekeepers could trade honey for turnips. At the market, a craftsman could barter products for food, supplies, and perhaps even a few coins.

Sir Guy was the local **judge.** He held a court for most crimes and decided all disputes: theft, fence boundary arguments, business deals, fistfights, and broken promises.

BUSINESSMAN & MERCHANT & JUDGE

Like a **banker,** Sir Guy brought cash into the community, paying for plows, farm tools, building supplies, armor and swords, and other imported stuff with rents and property taxes his sheriff collected from his landholders. He also got a cut of all the sales on market day. Many peasants didn't have coins; instead, they paid in barter—chickens, apples, cheese, onions.

Sir Guy was a **sportsman,** and it was fun, but hunting and fishing were serious business. Wild deer, rabbits, ducks, geese, fish, turtles, boar, and bear were important sources of food. The knight kept a big part of his land as forest, and balanced his needs for game and firewood.

BANKER & SPORTSMAN

Sir Guy the **investor** put money into large projects that could make a profit. He might build a bridge across a river and charge travelers a coin to cross it. He might build watermills, windmills, pottery ovens, or iron-working furnaces.

Sir Guy the **planner** was always worrying about winter. How harsh and how long would the winter be? How many stacks of firewood were needed to heat the big hall in the castle where food was cooked and everyone slept? How many candles were needed for the long winter nights? How much preserved food, flour, fruits, herbs, and oil would be needed?

INVESTOR ET PLANNER

just how fair were those ladies?

They were called "fair" ladies because their skin was pale. Noblewomen didn't do much real work, so they were seldom outside in the sun and wind. Noble wives and sweethearts were "protected" and kept at home, far from trouble. They were also kept far from authority and individual rights.

Noblewomen were seen more as dolls than serious people. Even "courtly love" was more about knights sighing and rolling their eyes than about partnerships.

Not every woman of the Middle Ages was a creampuff. Peasant women weren't pale, because they worked hard alongside their men. But because of the difficulties of childbirth and disease, they usually died young. There were also some feisty noblewomen who defended castles and managed estates when their husbands were away. There were even a very few tough queens. Knights ignored these examples and preferred the pale, silent babes.

A fair lady of noble birth walked above the filth and mud of the street on pattens, wooden clogs that protected her fine leather shoes. She used a walking stick to steady her on the rough cobble street, and she carried a pomander (a scent ball) to cover the stench of animals, poop (the streets were the only sewers), and people. Smells were believed to carry disease. Peasant women were too busy and too poor to be disgusted by the smell.

did knights slay dragons?

Dragons, like most legends, have some truth lurking around them. A religious basis for dragons was the evil serpent in the Bible's Garden of Eden.

Even before the Middle Ages, travelers had brought back tales of enormous serpents in India—some pythons are nearly thirty feet long. Could the spitting cobra have been the source of "fire-breathing" dragons? One dragon model was surely the African crocodile, more dangerous and deadly than most imaginary creatures.

To convince the gullible, there were "monster makers" who sewed together bits of several animals. These "baby dragons" were a favorite exhibit at country fairs. St. George and the dragon? Early Christian knights wanted to announce that they were just as brave as Vikings and barbarians. Slaying a dragon (wow!) made the point.

ou can't. To become a knight, you had to be able to trace your family's history back through five generations of "noble" ancestors, and even that wasn't enough. You needed influential friends—a duke or a king would be good. You also had to have money. Because a warlord needed armies, he might give sections of his own territory to new knights. Then they could make enough money to put together an army for him. The king had given land to the warlord for the same reasons. Knighthood was about land, power, and war.

Some knights took their pledge to the Church seriously. But for many, knighthood was a license to kill and rob.

Knights were a problem for the Church because they were powerful, made their own laws, were well armed, and were usually in a dangerous mood. It made sense for the Church to crowd in and regulate the knighthood business.

Devotion to the Church and Christian principles became part of the job. New knights prayed all night over their swords and armor and promised to be virtuous . . . while they were killing people. The Peace of God was a strict rule: Knights couldn't attack unarmed people, rob peasants or poor people, rob churches, destroy mills or vineyards, or attack anyone on their way to or from church. Common people were happy about this rule. The Truce of God forbade battles on holy days, saints' days, and any time between Thursday sundown and Monday sunrise. This left less time for pandemonium.

sounds good! how can I become a knight?

PAGE

If your papa had friends at court, and if your breeding was especially noble for generations, you might be accepted as a page. You ran errands and served meals for noble folk. You learned the elaborate formal manners of a court. In time, you might become a squire, an apprentice to a knight. Your training in horsemanship and weapons began. You cared for your knight's weapons and clothes and everything else. You might go with him into battle.

18

The **QUINTAIN** was a wooden dummy with a swinging weight for practicing horseback charges with a lance.

SQUIRE

The **PEL** was a simple wooden post used to practice the overhand, sidehand, and underhand cuts in broadsword fighting.

A new knight was "dubbed" by his lord or by the king. This was a light blow with a hand or with the flat of a sword, usually on one or both shoulders. This symbolized "waking the knight up" to his new work of supporting his warlord, the king, and the Church.

LAW AND ORDER in the hands of privileged, heavily armed, poorly educated warriors with almost limitless local power? Looking back, it doesn't sound like a great idea. Abuses of power were common. If a knight was the local authority and judge, who would arrest him? On the rare occasions when a knight was charged with a crime, he wasn't even judged by a jury of local citizens; knights could only be judged by other knights or lords higher on the feudal ladder. This was only one reason the Middle Ages was hard on peasants and short on justice.

Robert
the Bruce

Earl
of Oxford

Sir Hugh
Arbuthnott

heraldry

Bright symbols began as a way to manage troops during battles. A knight leading his little army wore something that his soldiers could see easily to stay close to him in the confusion. Since his troops seldom could read, symbols and combinations of color worked best. A knight might even wear a tall plume of feathers in the same way some drivers put ribbons on their cars' aerials: something to recognize across a mass of things. Later, the symbols were more about family connections. The battle umpires—heralds—recorded family symbols used on shields and crests (helmet decorations) with a rigid system of colors and graphics. Like much of knighthood, heraldry became more about who you were than about what you could do.

Sir Guy's home was his castle, but he didn't own it. It was owned by the king, because a castle was much more than a home. It was also part of a defense network.

If Burbank the Viking invaded, castles would be a problem for him. Each was the headquarters of a small army. If Burbank passed up Sir Guy's castle, Guy's army might attack him from behind. If Burbank stopped to attack, Sir Guy would button up and force the Viking to lay siege—to surround the castle and try to seize it by climbing the wall with ladders, throwing big stones, digging under its walls, or bribing the guards. This would take time. The armies from castles run by Sir Robert, Sir Patrick, and Sir David would take that time to join forces and attack Burbank from behind.

At the alarm for an attack, peasants hurried to get inside the castle's bailey with their cattle. The bailey had a water well and a comfortable stock of food for man and beast. The gates closed; the castle was buttoned up for a siege. How long a siege? For a hit-and-run raider like Burbank, a few days was too much trouble. But sieges lasting months were organized to conquer great castles and walled cities. It depended on how valuable the castle, the city, or its contents were.

*Most of the time, the castle was a **center of life.** Villages and great churches grew around its walls. The weekly market and seasonal fairs were held there. Castles were the seeds of cities.*

did knights live in castles?

*An important thing to remember about castle life is that nearly everything stopped after dark. It was a world **lit only by candles,** torches, and fireplaces—dim and inconvenient. The bulb in your refrigerator is brighter than anything castle folk had.*

ARROW SLIT

DRAWBRIDGE

A castle's walls were high and surrounded by a dry or a wet moat, so that a wheeled siege tower couldn't be pushed up against the walls. Castle gates were massive. Some had drawbridges across the moat and portcullises, heavy iron grilles that slid down and locked. Walls were topped with crenellations— spaced openings that allowed archers to peep out and shoot arrows. They could also shoot from arrow slits in the walls.

In case you wondered, castle folk relieved themselves in jakes, or necessaries. These wooden outhouses hung on the outside of castle walls. If the wind was blowing, stuff blew against the walls and stained them, but it was an ingenious way to keep the castle clean (inside, at least). At night, folks used chamberpots, big pottery pots with lids and handles. The pots were emptied out the window in the morning.

CRENELLATIONS

JAKES

PORTCULLIS

WELL

Holes in ceiling for dropping nasty things on invaders

Cells for prisoners, dark and damp

Secret exit for escape if castle was overrun

who's who in the castle?

There were castles and then there were CASTLES. A small castle might be home to a knight, some servants, and a few dozen men-at-arms (that is, paid soldiers). A duke's or a king's castle might house hundreds of knights and hundreds of people important to the life of the castle. Sir Guy's castle isn't large, but he has dozens of people working for him. You may recognize some of the names.

The **porter** is Sir Guy's chief guard of the gates and entrances (the ports). He answers the door.

Messengers carry Guy's official papers, orders, and letters. There is no post office. This is difficult work and could be dangerous. One duke didn't like a message he received and made the messenger eat the whole thing—wax seal, ribbon, parchment, and all.

The **marshal** watches over Guy's stables. He sees that hay and oats are stored, axles greased, horses brushed, and saddles repaired, and that those pesky grooms are kept busy.

The **sheriff** is Guy's shire reeve, an official of the shire (the lord's land). He collects rents and taxes. Not a popular guy.

The **butler** manages the beer and wine, kept in big barrels called butts.

Huntsmen are Sir Guy's favorites, his professional hunting guides for the forest. Only Sir Guy is allowed to hunt there. This was a sore point for lots of people and probably the beginning of forest-outlaw legends (like Robin Hood). Sir Guy sometimes allows peasants to hunt small game like rabbits, squirrels, foxes, and some birds.

The **chaplain,** a priest, keeps Sir Guy's chapel, where Guy and Edith hear holy mass each morning. He is the keeper of Guy's seal, an intricate engraving pressed into melted wax dripped on documents, something like a hard-to-counterfeit signature. He also writes Guy's letters for him, either in French (the language of the nobility) or in Latin (used by the Church).

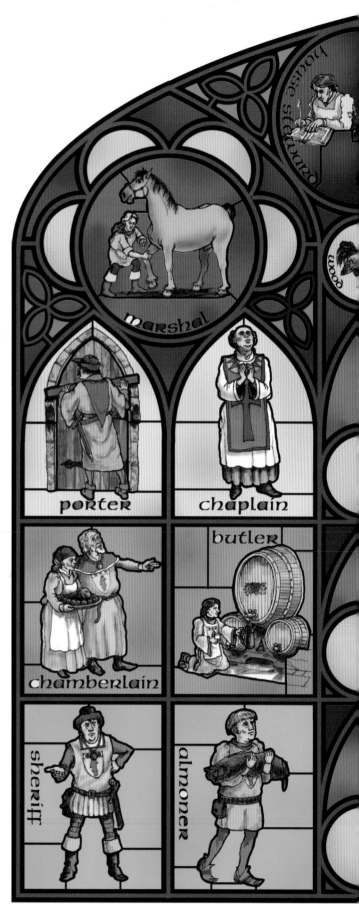

22

The **almoner** arranges Sir Guy's charity. Giving alms, or gifts, to the poor was a religious duty and a good way to keep the peasants happy. Old clothes, table scraps, and small purses of money go to widows, orphans, sick workers, prisoners, and old folks.

Stewards are managers. The house steward works with Lady Edith managing the castle's staff of servants, cooks, butchers, bakers, brewers, cleaners, seamstresses, and laundresses. Sir Guy's estate steward is old Sir William. He handles the complex business of the lord's expenses and his income from rents, taxes, sales, and fines. Sir William regularly visits every home, field, and shop. He sells wool, hides, flour, and produce, and he buys supplies. He is expected to report the estate's profits and losses every Michaelmas (September 29th).

The **chamberlain** is in charge of the great hall (or chamber). He has to be an authority on manners at the lord's table. Who gets served first? Who sits next to Sir Guy? Like other clever chamberlains, he is also Sir Guy's treasurer.

The **austringer** trains and keeps Sir Guy's falcons. Catching small game and birds (pheasant, ducks, even cranes) with fierce hawks and eagles was a popular sport. Training a wild animal to hunt for you is among the most difficult challenges, requiring patience beyond belief.

The **cofferer** is Guy's professional tough guy. He guards Sir Guy's chests (coffers) holding gold and silver.

OUTSIDE THE CASTLE there are two kinds of peasants: villeins and freeman.

Villeins own no land of their own but are not permitted to move away from their assigned fields. They work two or three days each week for Sir Guy. They're almost slaves.

Freemen own land. They can raise crops and cattle and make a profit. Some freemen are craftsmen who pay their lord in coin or trade their services as a kind of license.

The **blacksmith** is a freeman who cuts wood and builds earthen kilns in the lord's forest to make charcoal for his forge. In return, he shoes the lord's horses and makes iron tools and weapons for him. He forges iron tools for the village on his own time.

The **carpenter** cuts wood from Guy's forest in return for making and mending Guy's furniture or fixing his plows and wagons. He also builds homes, furniture, and farm equipment for the village.

The **miller** grinds the grain in Sir Guy's watermill. He takes a part of the flour for himself and a part for the lord as a tax. Since he does all the measuring, the villagers always accuse him of cheating.

The **wood hen** is part of a traditional Christmas bargain villagers make with Sir Guy. In exchange for a chicken, the villagers are allowed to gather dead branches for firewood in the forest. Sir Guy and Lady Edith get tired of chicken around Christmas.

edieval warfare is difficult for us to understand. There were no countries or governments to fight for. Most wars were vague land disputes between distant lords high up the feudal ladder. In one of these noble wars, a battle wasn't a single event: It was one battle for the nobility, and an entirely different battle for the peasant men-at-arms.

A knight went into battle to increase his reputation (so his lord might give him more land). He rode off well armored, well armed, on a trained horse.

A peasant risked everything out of simple obligation to his knight. He charged on foot, carrying a sword or pike. Perhaps he had a helmet and even some bits of armor. His view from the mud was probably less thrilling than the knight's view from horseback.

But even for armored knights, battle was dangerous. If a knight was pulled from his horse, infantrymen could swarm over them. And there was a deadly wild card on the battlefield.

enough castle business! what about those big swords?

BATTLEAXE

BROADSWORD

BATTLE HAMMER

MACE

Technology changed in the ninth century with the stirrup. It was a logical way to stick on the horse better. With the stirrup and improved saddles, horsemen had a more stable "seat" for swinging a sword or pointing a lance. This suggested a new battle group for knights: heavy cavalry—armored knights charging in a line. Historians insist that heavy cavalry changed warfare. Maybe, maybe not.

Knights were more interested in reputation than tactics. All the glory came from fighting other knights. Fighting peasants didn't impress lords and ladies. For knights, battle became a game. It even had umpires—an international brotherhood of battle observers, called heralds, recorded the fighting and kept score. Dead and wounded noble-men counted. Peasants didn't.

Arrows stuck in the ground. Armies carried thousands of arrows for their archers.

the wild card

The **archer** was the deadliest man on the medieval battlefield. His weapon looked simple but was a highly evolved killing machine: the longbow. Shaped from a stave of yew wood, it could throw a clothyard, a thirty-six-inch arrow, more than 300 yards. One archer couldn't hit a barn at that distance. But line up three dozen archers shooting at the same barn, and the barnyard becomes unfriendly. Archers could shoot six well-aimed arrows every minute. Accounts of medieval battles say that "arrows darkened the sky." It's possible. At 150 to 200 yards the iron-pointed arrows could puncture all but the thickest armor. Horses were lightly armored; they went down in the first flights of arrows, putting their knights on foot.

No infantry weapon was deadlier until the Civil War rifled musket. But paying any attention to archers seemed inglorious to knights. They were only peasants, after all. Knights kept charging in armored masses and went down like cut wheat.

On October 25, 1415, King Henry V and about 6,000 Britons were confronted by almost 20,000 French knights and infantrymen near the castle village of Agincourt. The French knights, eager for glory, charged again and again through mud and rain. At day's end, the French had lost as many as 10,000 men, plus a thousand taken as prisoners. The British, with their ranks of archers, were calm and methodical behind hedgehogs. They lost fewer than 200 men. The stupefying loss didn't change heavy cavalry tactics a bit. It was all about glory.

A line of armored knights thundering toward you might be impressive. But heavy cavalry was not effective against experienced foot soldiers. Hedgehogs, lines of sharpened stakes slanted toward the enemy, could prevent the cavalry from reaching the foot soldiers. Long pikes could keep knights at a distance or hook them from their horses.

Crossbows appeared in the thirteenth century. They were accurate but expensive, and they required long training. Their rate of fire was only about two arrows every minute.

One reason Sir Guy hates his lord's battle games is the bother of putting on armor. It takes at least an hour of fussing for his squire to suit him up. Some pieces tie to his padded under-suit. Many pieces are jointed and interlocked with other sections of armor like a jigsaw puzzle. Guy goes to the restroom before he puts it on.

Could they walk in this stuff? They walked, they ran, they jumped. The whole thing weighed only thirty to sixty pounds, distributed evenly over the entire body. It was so cleverly jointed that Sir Guy could almost play soccer in it. (They did play an early version of soccer, called football.) Armor was one of the marvels of medieval engineering.

how did they walk around in all that armor?

Armor had already been around for thousands of years by Sir Guy's time. Ancient warriors wore helmets and breastplates of bronze. Like later Roman soldiers, they might protect their forearms, hips, and shins with hard leather armor (boiled in oil or beeswax). Strips of metal were sometimes sewn into the leather.

Scale armor had small pieces of metal sewn, like overlapping fish scales, onto a flexible leather or cloth garment.

Plate armor held off some damage from heavy maces and battleaxes. By the fifteenth century, wealthy warriors wore plate armor in full top-to-toe suits. This is the armor in which we picture all knights, but it arrived late in the game.

MAIL

SCALE ARMOR

Mail was metal cloth made of joined rings of iron or steel, tailored like a metal sweater into a long shirt (a hauberk or birnie). A hood (or coif) was sometimes fastened to a conical metal helmet (or helm), which might have a protective piece over the nose (the nasal). To cushion hard blows, a padded tunic (a gambeson) was worn under the mail.

PLATE ARMOR

did knights joust?

Not seriously. *The notion of knocking another knight from his horse with a twelve-foot wooden stick was invented by Leopold VI of Austria late in the twelfth century as a spectator sport. Jousting had as much to do with medieval warfare as baseball.*

During the Middle Ages, war games called tournaments were social events. Teams of knights fought mêlées (MAY-lays)—mock battles on horseback. Pairs fought on foot with swords. Later, jousts were held on a measured field. Heavy jousting armor had a metal clip under the right arm to hold the enormous blunt lance. The jousting saddle had a high front and back. The knight was nearly bolted onto the horse. There were so few "falls" that the game was scored by how many wooden lances were broken.

It was like professional golf. Successful "athletes" made a lot of money on the tournament circuit. The victor won his opponent's horse and armor (they were usually bought back soon after). Only a few competitors got killed.

At first the Church banned tournaments, threatening to kick knights out of the Church (and heaven). But tournaments meant glory and money, so knights ignored the ban. The Church gave up during the fourteenth century, when it was were encouraging knights to join the Crusades.

"Crown" point—blunt for pushing, not piercing

Big silly decoration, probably for parades

Horse armor for the front

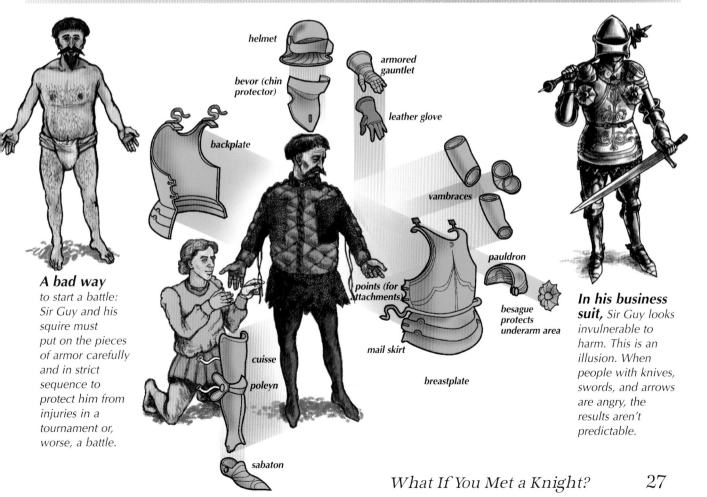

helmet

bevor (chin protector)

armored gauntlet

leather glove

backplate

vambraces

pauldron

besague protects underarm area

points (for attachments)

mail skirt

breastplate

cuisse

poleyn

sabaton

A bad way to start a battle: Sir Guy and his squire must put on the pieces of armor carefully and in strict sequence to protect him from injuries in a tournament or, worse, a battle.

In his business suit, *Sir Guy looks invulnerable to harm. This is an illusion. When people with knives, swords, and arrows are angry, the results aren't predictable.*

what were the crusades?

A journey to a holy place—a pilgrimage—was medicine for the soul. You might be forgiven for sins or crimes by making a religious journey. A holy destination for Christians, Jews, and Muslims was Jerusalem.

In 1009 the Muslim ruler of Jerusalem burned a big Christian church and roughed up some infidels ("unbelievers" in Islam). Pope Urban II called for a holy war to take back Jerusalem for the Christians. He said (in Latin), *"Deus vult!"* ("God wills it!") He promised that every "soldier of Christ" would be forgiven his sins. Each was to wear a cross (a *cruce*) on his tunic as a sign of his purpose: the Crusades.

For centuries, waves of knights, kings, and adventurers headed for the Holy Lands to defeat Muslim armies. There were also holy wars against Muslim Moors in Spain and even against fellow Christians—more than a dozen crusades over several centuries. Some knights joined out of faith, some out of greed, some wanted only adventure.

Every crusade was a disaster. Disease killed more than battles. Christian armies slew one another. Jerusalem was conquered for a few years but taken back by mighty Muslim armies. The Christian armies didn't have a chance: They were fighting in someone else's back yard, in unfamiliar deserts, directed by quarreling leaders. The only

28

Jews *in the Middle Ages were treated terribly. They were essential to European life as money-lenders, metalworkers, and merchants, but were officially despised. Most had no legal rights. They kept their own faith and customs within close-knit groups, and this seemed even more suspicious to Christians. Jews were blamed for plagues and wars. They were expelled from many countries and even exterminated in some regions. Their survival as a people is a miracle. And a tribute to their strength.*

Europeans who profited were the shipping cities, like Venice, who overcharged "soldiers of Christ" for passage to the battlefields.

Some say that mixing with new cultures in Asia and Africa changed European ideas. Crusaders brought back new ideas to light up the Dark Ages a bit. Little kingdoms fought as allies; perhaps this made way for larger, more stable nations. Some say the Crusades set the stage for the Renaissance. Most see them as a long-running calamity that deepened the divide between Jews, Muslims, and Christians, bled the populations of Europe, and distracted leaders from real problems at home.

the children's crusade

The Middle Ages had an uncomfortable faith in religion and mystic "signs." Around 1212, two twelve-year-old boys had similar visions: Crusades had failed because the warriors weren't pure. Children's purity would magically give them victory. Stephen of Cloyes, a peasant boy, collected thousands of French children. Separately, Nicholas of Cologne attracted thousands of German kids.

Disease killed most of the children before they got to the Mediterranean. When Stephen's "crusade" got to the water, they expected it to part (it parted for Moses!). The pope told them to go home, but they were determined to go. Ship owners offered them free passage to Jerusalem. They boarded seven ships. Two sank. Children in the other five ships were sold as slaves to the Muslims of North Africa.

Nicholas and his pure band made it as far as Pisa, where they were also offered a free ride. They were never heard from again.

knights and lords

It's easy to look back across the hills of history and see the bright flash of tinsel instead of sweaty reality. It's tempting to believe the minstrel stories, even when facts get in the way. By the time the troubadours began singing about gallant knights and the Code of Chivalry, the age of the armored knight had already begun to fade. There never was a sweet, magical time "when knighthood was in flower." Knights were brutally practical warriors with the unpleasant job of waging iron war with blows and blood.

The Renaissance followed the Middle Ages in the fifteenth century. It was a time for kings and popes to look more closely at the structure of the world. Science and bookkeeping were gaining on folklore and superstition. The little kingdoms were blending into powerful nations. Those nations raised trained, professional armies. Leading them was a little less about glory and a little more about winning. The knight of the Middle Ages became an army officer, a leader of trained troops.

Castles, swords, armor, and arrows would be important for centuries. The quaint concept of "noble families" would hang on. Treachery would always be popular. But the feudal ladder faded, the importance of the local warlord diminished. Knights evolved into members of a national war team.

Knights today—dubbed by one of the few remaining kings or queens—are businessmen, actors, and rock stars. Most of them can read. Most are gentler and more understanding than knights of the Middle Ages. But the professional warriors who wore armor and swung broadswords make today's knights seem pale.

charlemagne

Charlemagne *was perhaps the most important man in the Middle Ages, the great example of a king-father of Europe. With constant warfare, he built a great empire out of a confusion of minor kingdoms and bandit tribes—from Spain to the Baltic, from the Atlantic to the Rhine and beyond. He also created a working government reinforced by laws, learning, and communication. He was large of heart, but ahead of his time: His vast Frankish empire fell apart a generation after his death.*

henry II

Richard lionheart

sir william marshal

Henry II of England *was cunning, ruthless, intelligent, and the head of the Plantagenets, the most dysfunctional family in Europe. Henry married the beautiful and powerful Eleanor of Aquitaine and had eight children. All four of his surviving sons and his wife went to war against him several times. He forgave the sons and imprisoned the wife. The aggravation finally got to him; he died at fifty-six, but left a legacy of justice by laying the groundwork for English law.*

Richard I, the Lionheart, *though "Richard the Reckless" would be more accurate. Son of Henry II, Richard I was a mighty warrior but a derelict king. When crowned, he emptied the treasury and sold off titles to pay for a fruitless crusade. He was kidnapped by his allies while returning, and his subjects paid "a king's ransom" for his worthless hide. This king of England didn't speak English and spent only six months of his entire life there. Not interested in women, he left no heir. Brother John took over. Robin Hood was wrong: John was a better king.*

Sir William Marshal, First Earl of Pembroke, *was the best of knights, a warrior who was also loyal and wise. At age six, he was taken hostage while his father, John Marshal, was holding a castle against King Stephen. Stephen demanded that John open the gates, or, he said, he would hang the boy. John refused: "I have the hammer and the anvil to make even better sons!" But Stephen liked the kid and made him a page. As a knight, William made a fortune with his skills in tournaments, attracting the attention of Henry II, who made him tutor to "the young king," Henry III. When this teenage king died, William honored his dying wish: He went on crusade for two years. He returned as an adviser to Henry II. On the older king's death, he became adviser to Henry's rebellious son, Richard I, then to Richard's brother John. He became the Earl of Pembroke. He was a true knight in the best sense of the word.*

What If You Met a Knight?   31

sir guy of wareham

lived a long and active life and died at eighty-two. Old people were rare in the Middle Ages and respected for their toughness. He could have died of typhus, plague, dysentery, smallpox, tuberculosis, or infection from a simple cut—things we could cure today. He could have died in a famine or a Viking raid. When he was a young man he went on one of the Crusades; he could have died from a Muslim arrow or sword, but he broke his leg falling off a horse and returned to Wareham before any battles. He died of the flu in his own bed. He outlived Lady Edith, most of his friends, five kings, and all four of his children.

But he didn't outlive his grandchildren. He told them wonderful stories of chivalry and knighthood, lies he'd heard from troubadours, and the kids loved them. He never became a warlord, never had enormous lands. But he was loyal to his lords and his kings, and he took care of all the people on his land. When he died, his villeins and freemen and fellow knights wept. The freemen, with a penny here and a pound there, commissioned an effigy—a statue for his tomb in Our Lady of Tides. He was a brave, honest, trustworthy, practical knight, much nobler than a troubadour singing about fanciful chivalry could have imagined.

this book is for my knights

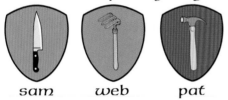

sam   **web**   **pat**

Copyright © 2006 by Jan Adkins
Published by Roaring Brook Press.
Roaring Brook Press is a division of Holtzbrinck
Publishing Holdings Limited Partnership,
143 West Street, New Milford, Connecticut 06776

Library of Congress Cataloging-in-Publication Data
Adkins, Jan. What if you met a knight? written and illustrated by Jan Adkins.
   p. cm.
Includes index.
ISBN-13: 978-1-59643-148-5
ISBN-10: 1-59643-148-2

1. Knights and knighthood—Juvenile literature. I. Title.
   CR4513.A46 2006
   940.1088'355--dc22   2005029163

10 9 8 7 6 5 4 3 2 1

Roaring Brook Press books are available for special promotions and premiums. For details, contact:
Director of Special Markets, Holtzbrinck Publishers.
Edited by Laaren Brown. Art direction by John Grandits.
Printed in the United States of America
First edition August 2006

index